DR. ANNE

Gloria Swanson
&Virginia Ott

D0063242

AUGSBURG Publishing House • Minneapolis

*To all the
Rons and Eddies,
Marys and Jeans
who know and love
Dr. Anne Carlsen*

DR. ANNE

Copyright © 1979 Augsburg Publishing House

Library of Congress Catalog Card No. 79-50083

International Standard Book No. 0-8066-1705-5

Photos on pages 51, 54, 62, and 74 are by Grant Colling.

MANUFACTURED IN THE UNITED STATES OF AMERICA

Contents

IS ANYONE THERE?

Is anyone there?
Does anyone care?
Without someone to care in life
It just doesn't seem fair.

—Mary Bane, 1972

Preface

To Children

Everything we tell you in this book really happened. Only a few of the names have been changed. Of course, we imagined some of the conversations.

To Parents and Teachers

To tell the story of Anne Carlsen is no small task. To tell her story for children who run and laugh and play and tumble on the ground and climb a jungle gym—this is a challenge.

She was a happy child. She was a brilliant student. She is a great woman. One honor after another has come her way. Her talents have been shared around the world. She is a beautiful example of what faith in God and self can do for others.

We wanted to write about Anne Carlsen in such a way that children who read her story will feel they have made a new and good friend.

To Those Who Helped

Our list of those to whom we say "thank you" is very long—relatives, friends, teachers, parents, the school staff, and especially the students we have known the past seven years. Most of these people you will meet in the story. And thank you, Anne Carlsen, for sharing your life story.

Adventure in Spring

It was the first warm Saturday afternoon that spring. Four teenage boys slowly made their way through the woods to the bend in the James River. Finally they reached a narrow point of land jutting out into the river. Tall oaks and elms surrounded them. This was Horse Shoe Park.

"We've just got to make a dock!" Roger exclaimed. "We can't throw a line to the deep places in the river unless we can get out from the bank!" He swung his arm back, then pretended to cast a fishing line. He could already see the four of them fishing from a dock.

"How are we going to do that?" asked Ron.

"Well, we'll need wood, some long fence posts and tools—hammers, saws, hatchets, nails. Let's look around and see what we can find. C'mon, you guys! Scatter!" This was Roger, who would one day be a math teacher, giving the orders.

Harold laughed. "I get it! We'll build a dock on the bank here and then pull it into the water and pound in the posts! Great!"

Luck was with them that day and for several more Saturdays in the early spring of 1951. Workmen had sawed fallen logs and stacked them all over the park for use in the outdoor fireplaces. Hidden among the trees was an old shed, where they found a hatchet and six logs for posts. Around the point they found nails left by workmen and by hobos who slept in the park.

Gradually the dock took shape. The boys sharpened the posts at one end with the hatchet, then rolled them, one at a time, into the river. Standing to his waist in the water, Roger did the spacing. Finally the posts were pounded into the river bottom.

Ron and Harold, with their strong arms, nailed together the boards for the dock. Then the boys used short logs to slide the boards to the river. With ropes they pulled the finished dock onto the posts and laboriously nailed them down. Finally—a place they could sit to fish!

There were plenty of worms under the brush along the shore. Soon four teenage boys were casting lines for fat bullheads and fighting catfish. They even hoped for a northern pike.

A river in springtime is a moving challenge. Roger soon had another idea. "Hey, guys! Why don't we build a raft? A big one so we can all get on it at the same time. Then we can really fish!"

"That would be neat! But Dr. Carlsen would never let us do that!" Harold shook his head. He was always cautious.

"We won't tell her or anybody else. It will be a secret!"

The secret took shape rapidly. They made a raft out of 13 small logs, held together with rope and planks they found in the shed. Then they rolled it on short logs to the water and tied it up to an old tree stump. Saturday would be the first voyage.

The next Saturday was a beautiful North Dakota day. The four boys quietly left their school dormitory and made their way to the river. It would not be easy to get all of them onto the raft. Two of them were in wheelchairs, one was on crutches, and one had a halting walk. But they were convinced they could do anything if they tried. After all, one of their school mottoes was, "Let me do it—it just may take a little longer."

Two of the boys pulled the raft close to shore. With much grunting and laughing and a great deal of pushing, pulling, and shoving, they managed to get Ron in his wheelchair onto the middle of the raft. He set the brakes on his chair so it would not roll off. With his strong arms he held the long pole they would use to push off from shore and move the raft up or down the river.

Then it was Harold's turn. No way could they push Harold's chair onto the raft. So Harold lowered himself out of his chair, then pushed and shoved and finally crawled onto the logs. Harold took the other long pole. Next came the fishing poles, worms, and a few dough balls.

Soon all four boys were on the raft. Harold shoved off from shore. Slowly the raft reached the middle of the river. It turned gently in the moving current and started slowly downstream.

"We did it!"

"It floats!"

"Wow! This is the life!"

They poled downstream a short way, fishing. Then they poled back and tied up to the tree stump. It took a long time for the boys to get back on solid ground, but they had a string of bullheads to give to the cook for supper. And that ride on the raft was worth all their efforts.

For several weeks the boys enjoyed their secret. Then came the last Saturday in May—a gorgeous, warm, blue-sky day. But for the boys this day would not go as planned.

They did not see Dr. Carlsen watching them as they left the school dorm and headed for the woods. She smiled, but her eyebrows were raised.

The boys pushed Harold in his wheelchair out onto the dock so he could pull himself onto the raft. But they let go of the chair too soon! Harold made it onto the raft, but his beautiful wooden wicker chair rolled off the dock into the deep water. It sank below the surface and settled in the mud.

What could they do? They couldn't pull the chair out of the water, and Harold couldn't get back to school without it. They decided they could face that problem later.

They poled downstream, farther than they ever had gone before. The birds were chattering spring songs. The trees were glistening with new leaves. The fish were biting. The boys didn't talk about the sunken chair. They all knew, though, that now Dr. Carlsen would find out about their secret.

When the sun was almost overhead, they poled back upstream to the dock.

"For pete's sake! Look at all those people!"

"And there's Dr. Carlsen, even!"

"How could she find out so soon?"

"Oh, boy! Now we're in for it!"

"Well," said Roger with a big sigh, "she al-

11

ways says, 'Go ahead and try.' We did, and it sure has been fun! Till now!"

The boys did not know that a woman living downstream had been looking out her kitchen window and had seen them on the raft. She could scarcely believe her eyes! A wheelchair on a raft in the middle of the river! She had called the school. And now almost all the staff members were waiting at the dock.

Harold was the spokesman. Before they reached the dock he began to explain. "Dr. Carlsen, I'm sorry about the wheelchair. But we're not sorry we made the raft. And we made the dock, too! It's been great!"

"Boys," laughed Dr. Carlsen, "I'm proud of your handiwork. It is indeed beautiful." Then she was very serious. "I will still see you all in my office immediately after lunch! The men will help you anchor the raft. One of them has already gone for another wheelchair for you, Harold."

The boys looked at one another and breathed sighs of relief. Dr. Carlsen understood. She was OK!

This woman who was OK is Dr. Anne Carlsen, administrator of the Crippled Children's Hospital-School of Jamestown, North Dakota. To the students, who come from all over the United States, she represents a goal. She is living proof that their lives can be successful and happy.

Dr. Carlsen is handicapped herself. How did this woman earn the title of "doctor" and become head of a school? She would say it was because, from the moment she was born, her father thanked God for her and promised loving care.

The Beginning

On a cold November night in 1915, everyone was excited in the Carlsen home in Grantsburg, Wisconsin. A baby was coming!

There were four brothers and a sister already. They had all been sent to the neighbors. Only Father, Mother, Dr. Bunker, and a nurse were in the house.

Little Anne was born early the next morning. The four grown-ups cried when they looked at the tiny baby. She was beautiful, but she had only short stubs for arms and no hands at all. One of her legs was very short, and the other was all twisted.

Alfred Carlsen took the baby in his strong hands and held her in his arms. He looked at his wife and said, "We shall wrap our love around this baby girl. With the help and understanding of her brothers and sister and of our

14

good doctor and neighbors, she will have a chance for happiness. We will thank God for this new life. I do believe he has something in mind for her."

Dr. Bunker told his wife about the new Carlsen baby later that day.

"Oh, how sad!" she cried. "Maybe she won't live!"

"My dear," the doctor replied, "of course she will live! She has a right to live. She may be a blessing to us all. She is a challenge to me! You and I and this whole town will help the Carlsens give their baby girl a chance for a happy life."

From the moment of her birth, Anne was indeed surrounded by a loving family and a compassionate community. Later she would say that this love made all the difference.

During that first winter people saw the baby wrapped in blankets. She looked like a blue-eyed doll. As she grew, Anne began to use her short arms—to feed herself, to pick up toys, to toss a ball. She would push and shove herself along, showing her family she could do what they could do. They applauded whenever she did something for the first time.

The Carlsens were a close, loving family. Clara, the older sister, did much of the housework because Maren, their mother, was not well. But Clara still found time to play with baby Anne and to read her stories. The brothers—Frank, Darvey, Richard, and Albert—also helped at home.

Their love and concern for one another helped the family through a sad time. When Anne was only four years old, her mother died. Clara was 13. She became the substitute mother in the household. She was always busy cooking, washing, ironing, mending, cleaning, and, of course, doing her schoolwork.

Anne was cared for by neighbors while the boys and Clara were at school. But after school and on weekends, when the brothers went out to play, Anne went along. They never let her out of their sight.

The Carlsens had a big backyard where neighbor children played. Anne was included in every game, especially Pum-Pum Pullaway and Prisoner's Base. Her favorite game was baseball. She liked to be catcher. Of course, there had to be a few special rules when Anne played.

While watching Anne pull her strong body around the shortened bases, Alfred Carlsen had an idea. That very day he went to the hardware store to buy a kiddie car. The front wheel of the kiddie car was attached to handles that could be guided by very short arms. The seat was low and flat and set above the rear wheels. It would not easily tip over.

In a very short time Anne had figured out how to sit on the kiddie car and propel it with one leg, steering with her short arms. This was just what she needed! Now she could move fast! No longer did the bases have to be shortened when Anne came to bat. And someone was always ready to push her around the bases or up and down the sidewalks as fast as they could run. Such fun!

Dr. Bunker smiled as he saw Anne, on her kiddie car, flying down a hilly street past his office. "With the right device that girl could walk, maybe even run!" he thought.

He was always thinking of some way to help her. Now he began wondering where he could send Anne to have an artificial leg made. Probably the children's hospital in Madison, Wisconsin. But Anne must be a little older.

"Little Anne has the heart of an athlete," said the good doctor, "but she wants things too fast."

One day he had another idea. "Anne, I have a surprise for you! I know something you will be able to do as well as any other child. If it does not rain tomorrow you and I will go to the lake."

Next day the sun was shining. Dr. Bunker and his wife picked up Anne and took her with them to Mudhen Lake.

"Here we are! Now put on this bathing suit. I want to see if you are part fish."

That afternoon Anne had her first swimming lesson. By the end of the summer Anne could swim.

"Now you can do something as well as or even better than other children," Dr. Bunker said proudly to his student.

Anne laughed. "Then does that mean that I'm part fish?"

Happy Birthday

When Anne's sixth birthday came, something happened that changed everything. That "something" was a present she received, a five-dollar check.

Anne did not understand a check. She had never been to school, and she could not read or write. She picked up the check and took it to her brother.

"Darvey, what is this piece of paper for?" asked Anne.

"That, my small pumpkin of a sister, is a check. It is worth five whole dollars. All you have to do is write your name on the back of it and you can have five dollars to spend." Darvey's eyes began to shine as though he had an idea.

"But, Darvey, I can't write my name!" cried the little girl.

"Now that you are six years old, it's time you learned! And I'm just the one to teach you. Get up here on this chair at the table and I will give you your first writing lesson."

Quickly Darvey placed a tablet and a pencil before Anne.

"Now put this pencil between your arms the way you hold your spoon, only point it down to the paper. I'm going to write your name and leave a space underneath for you to copy it. Then I'll write it again and you can copy it again."

Over and over Anne traced her name and tried to copy it. This was hard work for her short arms. For the next few days everyone in the family helped Anne learn to write her name. Finally the great day came! Anne could proudly write her name without even looking at Darvey's copy.

That same day she went to the Grantsburg bank. She slowly wrote "Anne Helen Carlsen" on the back of that check. Her eyes sparkled as the bank teller counted out five crisp one-dollar bills.

For Anne, learning to write her name was just like finding the key to a treasure chest. She must learn to write and to read other words. There were many books in the Carlsen home. The boys and Clara brought home their school-books. Anne looked in all of them. She was always saying, "What's this word?" Then she would copy it carefully, repeating the word over and over.

Her father saw how excited Anne was about learning. Looking into her sparkling eyes as she pointed to yet another word, he thought about Anne's intelligence. Her bright little mind must be trained!

In those days most handicapped children were kept at home and sometimes even hidden away. Their families or hired help cared for them all their lives. Seldom did parents even think of sending a crippled child to school. But Mr. Carlsen could see that the answer to Anne's handicap was education.

One evening he picked up Anne and held her on his lap. He tousled her blonde hair and said, "Anne, dear, I'm proud of the way you are learning. Keep it up! You know, two arms and two legs missing aren't as important as one head present. The best way to make that head help the most is to get it educated. I must soon see to this! I will visit the school."

In the spring when Anne was seven years old, her father went to see the principal of the Grantsburg school. "Our Anne is truly ready to go to school. Will you let her come next fall? Her brothers will look out for her before and after school."

The principal hesitated. How could a child

as crippled as the Carlsen girl be bright enough for school? But then the principal smiled and said, "I know you all love her dearly, and you wouldn't want her to come to school and feel out of place. We will first give her an intelligence test to see if she is able to learn. Then we will talk about her coming to school."

One day soon Mr. Carlsen took Anne to the school to be tested. Question followed question, some much too difficult even for children who had been to school. One of the last questions was, "Who was Longfellow?"

Anne knew nothing about the poet Longfellow, but she did know a long fellow. With a big smile she answered, "That tall, tall policeman downtown. He is a long fellow!"

Anne passed the intelligence test with a high score. If the principal still had doubts about Anne learning in school, he did not tell the little girl and her father.

"Let her try school. She can come the last two months this term, and if it goes well she can then come full time next fall."

The principal and Mr. Carlsen were indeed ahead of their time to encourage a severely handicapped child to attend a public school. Because her father was determined that Anne have an education and because a principal was willing to let her "try school," Anne entered first grade when she was seven years old.

School Days in Grantsburg

Getting Anne to school became a family project. Each morning one of her brothers pulled Anne in a wagon up the hill to school. Then he carried her up the steps to her school room. There Anne kept a kiddie car, so she could go up and down the halls with the other children. Anne and her kiddie car were a familiar sight for several years in the Grantsburg school.

That first school year was so exciting! Not only did Anne get a small taste of reading and writing, she was around other children her own age. She had to make new friends. This, too, was a kind of test.

The teachers were amazed at how rapidly she learned. She passed two grades of school in that first year. When summer came, she was in a hurry for fall to arrive so she could be in third grade.

But the year she was nine, Anne did not go to public school. Dr. Bunker had other plans for his favorite patient. He talked to Anne and her family.

"Anne must enter Wisconsin General Hospital in Madison for special surgery. There is a doctor there who can operate on Anne's right leg. He can straighten and strengthen the muscles around the knee so she can wear an artificial leg. It will help you to walk, Anne."

"But, Dr. Bunker!" Anne interrupted, "Can't I go to school and do that, too?"

"No, my dear, there won't be time for that because you must have lots of what we call therapy. There will be people who are especially trained to give you exercises to strengthen your legs. They will teach you how to walk."

Anne was sad. She was afraid her classmates would get ahead of her at school. They might even forget her! It is not easy to be nine years old and to be 400 miles away from home in a hospital for almost a year.

But a surprise was waiting for Anne when she got to that hospital. A teacher came right to her bedside! Anne was able to keep up with her reading and writing. And her classmates back home did not forget her. During all those

24

months of surgery and therapy, they sent her happy letters and cards.

While Anne was away, her father married again. Esther was an Iowa woman whose children from her first marriage were now grown and working away from home. She, too, wrote to Anne. She did not want them to be strangers.

One day in the spring Anne came home to Grantsburg. With help from her new crutches, she slowly walked on a leg-like device attached to her own short leg. It was clumsy and awkward. She could not sit down while wearing it. She stood at the table to eat her meals. She could not even ride her kiddie car.

Day after day Anne tried to wear the device, but it was just too slow. Anne Carlsen had to move faster!

"Father, please let me leave it off," she pleaded. "I can promise to wear it on Sundays, but for school and play I like my kiddie car and the new coaster wagon. Dr. Bunker will understand. I just can't get anyplace with this new leg!"

That fall Anne and the kiddie car went back to school. The students welcomed her. The boys all wanted to push her down the hall, so they took turns.

Each time Anne would say, "Don't go too fast! I can't steer around the kids and the corners unless you go a little slower." Although she didn't say so, Anne enjoyed getting a fast ride as much as the boys enjoyed giving her one.

Then one day it happened! They had just come in from recess. One of the boys pushed the kiddie car as hard as he could. At break-neck speed, Anne, the kiddie car, and boy raced down the hall to the third-grade room. They were both laughing so hard they did not notice the teacher standing in the doorway until it was too late to turn away. They ran right over the toes of the surprised teacher!

Anne was much quicker at learning than at turning. That year she again completed two grades. In fact, she completed two grades each year until, by the time she was 12 years old, Anne was ready for high school.

People in Grantsburg proudly watched Anne's progress in school. They marveled at the ease with which she learned, moved about, and took care of herself. But no two people were more proud than Anne's father and Dr. Bunker. They discussed Anne's future.

"Grantsburg has been good to our family. It has accepted Anne and given her a good start. But Anne will need more schooling than what she can get here," Mr. Carlsen said.

"And she'll be needing big city orthopedic specialists soon," added Dr. Bunker.

The Carlsens began making plans to move away from Grantsburg.

Alfred Carlsen had been born in the small country of Denmark. As a young man he worked as a gardener at the royal palace in Copenhagen. These royal gardens were some of the most beautiful in Europe, with flowers, hedges, shrubs, and ornamental trees. When World War I was about to break out, Mr. Carlsen emigrated to Wisconsin. He farmed a few years before he moved into Grantsburg. Then he bought a greenhouse and became a florist.

Mr. Carlsen's love for flowers led him now to a new job in St. Paul, the capital city of Minnesota, about 90 miles south of Grantsburg. He was hired as a gardener at Gillette Hospital, a famous hospital for treating crippled children. Here he would be doing just what he had done years before in Denmark.

Mr. Carlsen found a house just one block from St. Paul–Luther Academy, where Anne could go to school. Darvey and Anne were the only Carlsen children still at home. Mr. Carlsen was happy as he told them of his plans.

"Darvey, you will stay in Grantsburg and finish high school. I have made arrangements for you to earn your board and room by helping out at a nearby dairy farm. Anne, you and Esther and I are moving to St. Paul. We will live just one block from St. Paul–Luther Academy. You will be able to finish high school there and maybe go to junior college for two years right in that school! It is a church school. Everyone is certain to be kind to you."

Alfred Carlsen was much more eager to move than was Anne. She knew almost all of the 800 people in Grantsburg. They saw the friendly girl inside and did not notice the different body outside. She liked the tree-lined streets, the hills, the nearby lakes, and the beautiful St. Croix River.

Anne was worried. She confided to her old friend. "I know Dad is doing all this for me, Dr. Bunker, but it scares me to move to a strange, big city."

"It will be strange for you at first, Anne," he replied. "But, with your intelligence and spirit, you'll find it's the best place for you. We will miss not having you in Grantsburg, but you won't be that far from us, and we will never forget you. In fact, Anne, I expect to hear great things of you in the future!"

"Thank you for what you've done for me all these years, Dr. Bunker. I hope I won't disappoint you!"

New Home,
New Legs, New School

In the summer of 1928, 12-year-old Anne, her father, and her new mother moved to St. Paul. Anne was fitted with a leg brace, one artificial leg, and two artificial arms that summer. She soon learned to walk quite well with the new brace and leg, but the arms got in her way. She took them off and put them way back in the corner of her closet. She could get along just as well as anybody else with the arms she had!

When school began that fall, Anne was one of the 20 freshmen. She was the youngest in her class, and the shortest. "Do you still play with dolls?" one of her classmates asked.

"Of course not!" Anne was indignant. But she didn't say that she had just put her dolls away the summer before!

All the worries Anne had about moving from

Grantsburg seemed to come true during the first few weeks at Luther Academy. Strangers stared at her when she walked to school. Schoolmates were polite and kind, but they did not feel comfortable with Anne, nor did Anne feel at ease with them. She was lonesome for her friends back in Grantsburg.

"Back home I felt like everybody else and they all treated me as one of them," she told her father. "Now, for the first time in my whole life, I *feel* how different I look."

"They will forget your differences once they get to know you," Mr. Carlsen promised his daughter.

Pastor Schmidt, the head of the academy, and the teachers helped Anne to be patient, to give other students time to see what an enjoyable girl she was.

Then one day, soon after Anne's 13th birthday, a classmate asked Anne, "Why don't you write so I can read your notes?"

Anne laughed. The teasing question made her happy. Now she knew she was one of them. They liked her well enough to joke with her.

Anne soon had many friends. On warm sunny days they would go for walks, pushing Anne in her wheelchair. Sometimes they would go the three miles around Lake Phelan, which was near the school.

Anne had one very special friend she called

"my guardian angel." This girl brought books to Anne from the basement library. She helped Anne schedule her classes so she wouldn't have so many flights of stairs to climb. She also helped include Anne in student get-togethers.

Anne watched football and hockey games from a first-floor window. She joined several clubs and wrote her own column for the school paper. Her days became too busy and happy for her to feel lonesome for Grantsburg. Luther was her school now. St. Paul, Minnesota, was her home.

She often had trouble keeping up with the others. If only she could walk with her legs as fast as she could learn with her head!

When she was a junior the doctors at Gillette Hospital decided to take a radical step and operate again. This time Anne's left leg was amputated just below the knee. Now she would have two artificial legs, and she would be able to stand erect. With crutches she would soon be able to walk!

From November to March, Anne was hospitalized for the surgery and therapy. Again a bedside teacher helped her keep up with her classmates. She was not as lonely during this hospital stay because classmates came often to see her and to tell her what was happening at school. Best of all, her father came to see her every day she was there. Each time he

31

brought her a fresh flower which he had grown in the hospital's little greenhouse.

On the first day of school the next fall, a girl on crutches made her way into the building. What would the other students say now?

"Hey, kids! It's Anne! She's walking!"

They ran to meet her, and soon they were talking and chattering.

"It's great you're back!"

"Boy, did we miss you last year in Latin class!"

"How are you? Does it hurt to walk?"

Anne laughed. She was so happy! Of course it hurt to walk! But Anne could stand the pain. She was so glad to be back in school, working hard to catch up in her studies.

During the next year Anne finished high school. She and her father decided that, since she was doing so well at the academy, she should take two years of college there.

Anne's grades continued to be very high, and Dr. Schmidt encouraged her to finish college. She had to make a big decision. What college should she go to for her last two years?

Even her father, who long ago told a little girl he loved that her head must be educated, could not have foreseen that his daughter would now be climbing to the top in the academic world.

For a long time Anne had been thinking about what she would like to do all her life.

"Father, I want to do something to make my own living! What I really want to be is a teacher—English, maybe, in a high school. I know I couldn't chase the little kids, but I bet I could challenge the older ones. What do you think?"

"Anne, my dear, what I think is that you are an amazement to me! And what you want, I want you to try. Many people are going to tell you 'you can't!' this or that. Sometimes they may be right. Part of life is accepting what we can't change and then never being quite satisfied with the rest. Now, have you decided where you will go on to college?"

"Yes, Dad, I've thought about that, too. But it was the kids in our neighborhood who really helped me make up my mind."

"How did they do that?"

"Well, many of them are going to the University of Minnesota, and they're going to drive back and forth each day. They said I could go with them. You wouldn't have to drive me, and it would be an inexpensive way to go. Besides, the U is a great school for training teachers!"

University Days

Now that Anne had decided where to continue college, she was impatient to get started. That summer she studied the university catalogs and made lists of the courses she hoped to take that fall. One Sunday afternoon Clara drove Anne all around the sprawling university campus so she could see where her classes would probably be.

Such a big school! Anne could barely count all the buildings. They drove past old, vine-covered Folwell Hall, where Anne knew some of her classes would meet. "I suppose they'll be on the third floor!" she thought to herself.

Then they went by Burton Hall. Anne remembered she would have a class there, too. "It's a long way between those two buildings," she thought. "What if I have a class on the third floor of Folwell and the next class is way over here at Burton? Maybe I could save time by sliding down the banisters at Folwell!"

Anne sat up straighter. Why worry about it? Whatever obstacles came up, she would meet them head-on. "I wish school were starting tomorrow!" she exclaimed. She didn't want to wait another minute to begin learning to be a teacher.

On registration day the campus was covered with thousands of students hurrying to register for classes. "My legs will never keep up with them," Anne laughed to herself, "but maybe my head will!"

She was soon sitting at the table where education students were enrolling. After all, she was not a freshman. She'd already completed two years of college work. She was ready now to specialize her training.

Holding the pencil firmly with her two short arms, she filled in a schedule of the classes she wanted. She pretended that the secretary and a dozen others in the room were not watching her. The secretary took the completed schedule and said, "Please wait, Miss Carlsen. I think the head of our department will want to check this himself."

Through the office window Anne could sense them looking at her and checking her papers. Other students were not having their schedules checked. Anne could almost guess what was coming.

The young woman came to the door. "Please come in, Miss Carlsen."

The instructor stood up and cleared his throat. "Please be seated, Miss Carlsen. I see that you want to be a teacher?"

"More than anything!" Anne exclaimed.

"Well, I must say, your grades from high school and junior college tell me you are an excellent student and might become a good teacher. However. . . ."

Anne tried to look as confident as possible and not to show the disappointment she was already beginning to feel.

"The truth is, Miss Carlsen, this country is in the middle of a terrible depression. There are well-qualified teachers all over the country who can't find jobs. You see. . . ."

Anne thought to herself, "What he really means is that if teachers with arms and legs can't find work, I won't be able to."

Aloud Anne said, "You would not encourage me to become a teacher. What would you suggest that I study for?"

"Well, I . . . I really couldn't say. Why don't you go over to see Dr. Williamson? He's the head of our university counseling bureau. He has information on all kinds of jobs that are available. He might be able to give you some good advice about what classes to take."

Anne made her way to the third floor of Northrop Memorial, where she found Dr. Williamson. He watched her swing across the room on her crutches.

"I really want to be a teacher," Anne explained, "but the education department doesn't think much of that idea."

Dr. Williamson looked at Anne over the top of his glasses. He saw a pretty, alert face, blue eyes, and light, wavy hair. All her papers on the desk before him were filled out in longhand. He wondered how she could have done it. Then he smiled and spoke.

"Now, Miss Carlsen—I believe I will call you Anne—let's be realistic. You would find it difficult to be hired as a teacher. There are so few job openings and so many teachers already. But you must not be discouraged. With your splendid records, there must be a job for you somewhere."

Anne's spirits began to rise. She felt that here, in the middle of this huge university, was someone to whom she could bring her problems.

As the years went by, Anne found this to be true. Dr. Williamson told his secretary that whenever Anne came to see him, she was to let her in even if she didn't have an appointment. Through the years he was never too busy to talk to her. They became lifelong friends.

Soon after their first meeting, Dr. Williamson gave Anne a battery of aptitude and ability tests at upper-college level. They only confirmed what she already knew—that she had an aptitude for English literature, history, and creative writing.

At their next conference, Dr. Williamson asked, "Anne, what do you like to do better than anything else?"

"Read!" was her quick reply.

"Well, why don't you go ahead and major in English literature? You keep up the study part, and I'll work on the job part. There's a career for you somewhere!"

When she left Dr. Williamson's office, Anne made herself a new promise: "I'll take the literature and history and the writing, also. If I can't be a teacher, I'll be a librarian."

Anne studied hard, but she also had fun. There were so many things to do!—plays to see, concerts to hear, and, when she could afford it, wonderful athletic contests. Dr. Bunker used to say that Anne had the heart and spirit of an athlete. This fighting, winning spirit would help her enjoy all of life.

Anne Helen Carlsen was 20 years old when she was graduated from the University of Minnesota, cum laude (with honor). The first part of her great dream had now come true. She had a college degree! Now could she find a job and begin earning her own living? At the family gathering after commencement, Anne told her brothers and sister, "Father shouldn't have to work all his life for me. And I don't intend to let any of you do that either!"

But though Anne was ready for work, work was not available. The Great Depression still held the country in its terrible grip. Jobs were scarce and money was even scarcer. Laborers sometimes got one dollar a day. Teachers might get $50 a month. But Anne, with her usual optimism, tucked her Bachelor of Arts degree into the purse hanging from one crutch and swung out to meet the world of work.

Searching for a Career

Anne's first stop was at Walter Library on the university campus. She hoped to register for classes in library science and to get a job working part-time in the library.

The librarians knew Anne because she had often studied there the past two years. They respected her, but they did not hire her. Nor did they recommend that she register for classes.

"You know," they told her, "as a librarian you would have to start out carding books and putting them on shelves. Our stacks have steep steps and narrow aisles, which would be too difficult for you to manage. Librarians do not just sit at desks!"

Anne saw another career choice fall away. "Now where should I look?" she asked Dr. Williamson.

Every time he heard about a job opening suiting Anne's qualifications, Dr. Williamson told her. But no one seemed interested in hiring a handicapped person. Then one day he called Anne into his office.

"You know there are several publishing houses here in the Twin Cities. One of them needs a proofreader and another needs a writer. Good luck!"

Joy! Joy! Jobs she knew how to do and would enjoy! Anne hummed as she rode a streetcar to downtown St. Paul. "Publishing job, here I come!"

Once again her balloon of hope was punctured.

"I'm sorry, Miss Carlsen," the receptionist said. "This company's insurance policy will not allow us to hire any handicapped persons. You see, in case of fire it might be difficult for you to leave the building fast enough."

To herself Anne answered, "You just try me! I'm not as handicapped as you think." But she was gracious and polite to the receptionist.

Once again she put on her brave, self-confident face, lifted her chin, and went to the next publisher. Here she met the assistant editor. But the result was the same.

"Sorry, Miss Carlsen. You have excellent recommendations, but we are looking for someone more experienced and mature."

To herself Anne said, "You mean, someone who has two arms and two legs."

Anne told her brother Frank about these interviews. "I've decided that employers think legs and arms are more important than brains —even educated brains!'"

Then Frank had something to say. "Anne, I've been thinking, and the rest of the family agrees with me. We think you ought to go back to the university and study journalism. You always were good at writing. Maybe in a year or two there will be more jobs available. This depression can't last forever. I'll pay your tuition if you go back. What do you say?"

"Oh, Frank! I can't thank you enough! If I take your money, I'll pay you back every cent you loan me. I don't know when, but I will! My family is the greatest!"

Anne remembered another little girl in Wisconsin, crippled by polio when she was nine years old. She lived one mile from school, but her family didn't make the effort to educate her. She became an adult with only a child's education.

Anne's family made all the difference. She knew that one mile would not have stopped them. To school she went, and in school she succeeded. And now, once again, they were helping her.

One of the first people to find out Anne was

again at the university was Dr. Williamson. Once again he helped her arrange her classes, and he looked for work she could do to help with her expenses. Her first job was editing articles Dr. Williamson had written for magazines. She corrected and rearranged his writing, trying to improve his first draft. Two of the articles were published in a literary quarterly.

After only a few months back in school, Anne faced the second great sorrow of her life. Her adored father died. He had been her lifelong security, always there to encourage and bolster her spirits. Suddenly he was gone.

"From the time I can remember," Anne said years after his death, "my father encouraged me to think I could do anything I really wanted to. He was proud of my achievements—small as they might be. He was optimistic and had a great deal of faith in the goodness of God. He was gentle, kind, and intelligent. I wanted to succeed to please him."

The Carlsen home in St. Paul was closed. Esther Carlsen went to live with one of her older children.

Anne quit her classes at the university and went to live with Clara. Again the brothers came to her rescue. They bought her a typewriter. Then they made leather cuffs for her short arms. To each cuff they fastened a metal stem with a rubber tip. She typed out stories and articles and sent them to various editors. Only rejection slips came back.

Reading had always been Anne's favorite pastime. Knowing that a writer must first be a reader, she began reading a variety of things. She read again the short stories of Sherwood Anderson in *Winesburg, Ohio*. She read novels by F. Scott Fitzgerald and Sinclair Lewis. She read a short novel by John Steinbeck—an author on his way up. She read the poetry of E. E. Cummings. She liked Robert Frost and Carl Sandburg. They were men of the earth, as her father had been.

Once a month she went to the library just to read E. B. White's column "Talk of the Town" in the *New Yorker*. Anne also read novels by Grace Livingston Hill and Grace Richmond. Reading from the Bible, especially the New Testament, kept the faith and courage of her father ever before her.

In addition to reading, Anne did some baby-sitting. She kept herself busy, but it was harder and harder not to become discouraged.

Then one day Dr. Williamson called Anne. "Just heard about another local publisher who wants a proofreader. And I *checked!* They hire handicapped persons. So put on your best bib and tucker, or whatever you call woman's wear, and get over there. It's a church publishing house."

But Anne wasn't going to be in such a hurry this time. If this was a church-related job she wanted a recommendation from Pastor W. F. Schmidt, whom she had known at the academy. He was now head of the Religion Department at Concordia College in Moorhead, Minnesota. She called him that very day.

"I would be glad to give you a recommendation," the pastor said, "but, Anne, I thought you wanted to teach! Just today I recommended you for a teaching job at the Good Samaritan School for crippled children in Fargo. They need a high school teacher. I told the director, Mr. W. B. Schoenbohm, who is a friend of mine, that you were probably available. I hope you are. . . ."

"Available! I certainly am!" Anne almost shouted over the phone. "Oh, thank you, Prexy! I'll call Mr. Schoenbohm right away!"

Almost before she knew it, Anne was on the train headed for Fargo and a personal interview. Of course, she got this job. Who would be better for teaching handicapped children than a handicapped teacher?

It was 1938, and Anne Helen Carlsen had her first full-time, professional job. At last she was to be a *teacher!*

The Dream Comes True

Anne could scarcely believe that her dream had come true. A few times during those first weeks of teaching, she had to poke herself to see if she was dreaming. But when she received her salary after one month of classes, she knew she really was a teacher.

Anne was paid $25 a month. She also was given a room and meals. "Good Samaritan was a poor school. We ate a lot of soup," Anne remembers. But her small salary was enough to give her independence. She was now truly on her own. "If only Father could have lived to see my dream come true," Anne wrote to Clara.

Anne knew she wanted to spend the rest of her life teaching. However, since at the university she had been discouraged from becoming a teacher, she had not taken the courses required to earn a teaching license. Now Mr.

Schoenbohm helped Anne make arrangements to take classes in psychology and methods of teaching English at Concordia College, across the Red River. So Miss Carlsen, new teacher, was also a very busy student. When she had earned the official teaching certificate, her position at Good Samaritan was secure.

However, the struggling Good Samaritan School was not secure. It was decided that the school had little future. But the Lutheran Hospital and Home Society of America thought differently. This organization took over the school and rebuilt it 95 miles west in Jamestown, North Dakota.

During the year the new school was being built, Anne went back to Gillette Hospital in St. Paul, this time to teach at the bedsides of junior high students.

Then came the special day in 1941 when Anne went to Jamestown to the new Crippled Children's School on the banks of the James River. A small, second-floor apartment in the school was her home. She went up the stairs backwards—she said it was easier to fall that way. Her life centered around classrooms and students. She was happy.

But the longer Anne taught, the more she realized she had to know more about the problems handicapped children had in learning. Back to school she went. Anne spent four summers at the University of Northern Colorado at Greeley and earned a master's degree in education. The name of the study Anne did to earn this degree was "Reading for Therapy or Bibliotherapy," a method being used at Jamestown.

Still Anne kept going to school. She took a leave of absence and for two years she worked at earning her doctor's degree in education from the University of Minnesota. When she went back to Jamestown, she was made principal of the Crippled Children's School. In 1949 she earned that highest degree. Now she was Dr. Carlsen!

She became child guidance director at the school. In 1950, when Mr. Schoenbohm left, she became administrator. Her dream to be a teacher had come true in a bigger way than she had ever dreamed!

Anne thought back to a summer class at the university. One day another teacher sitting beside her had said to Anne, "If I were like you, I wouldn't want to live."

Anne smiled. Not want to live! Why not? Her handicap had not stopped her from becoming a teacher. It would help her now in showing physically handicapped children that they could learn to use their talents and abilities as well as anyone else.

A Special School

During Anne's first years of teaching, polio vaccine had not yet been developed. Summers were filled with fear as epidemics left children and adults with crippled legs and arms and backs. Lives were changed as active people suddenly found themselves in wheelchairs or on crutches.

Children crippled by polio were sometimes discouraged from going to school. "How could you possibly get up and down steps?" they were asked. Often parents who lived on farms didn't have ways to get their handicapped children to schools. Some young people didn't get a chance to go to school until they were almost grown up.

One such boy was Billy. He was 10 years old before his parents were able to enroll him in the Crippled Children's School. He became sad when he could not answer some of the questions in the test required for admission. "You know," he said, "I haven't been around much to learn things. Seems like I've spent more time in bed than in school ever since I started. And you can't learn stuff that way."

Another boy, crippled from polio when he was a baby, was left with useless legs and a crippled back. He was a teenager before he started school at Jamestown. Tests showed he had superior ability, but he had never been taught to read or write. In four years he completed eight years of school! After he graduated from high school he even went to college for a year. Then he took a class in watch repairing. With this trade he was able to find a job and support himself. "His whole life changed because there was a school he could attend," Dr. Carlsen says proudly.

Dr. Carlsen is proud whenever she sees her students find their place in the world where they can contribute and be independent. She watches them become teachers, accountants, mechanics, radio announcers, journalists—doing almost every job anyone else can do. She knows how hard they work to make people see that they, too, can do something worthwhile.

Today, because of its excellent extended services, the school is known as the Crippled Children's Hospital-School. Students come there

from every part of the United States and even
from other countries. The students have physical disabilities making it impossible for them to
attend regular schools. Many have speech and
hearing difficulties. Some have been born with
defects. Others are crippled from accidents.

More than half of the students have cerebral
palsy. This disease is caused from damage to
brain cells. Sometimes babies are born with
cerebral palsy. Infections, diseases, and accidents can also cause it. Those who have it cannot be cured because damaged brain cells can
never be repaired. But most of these people
can be taught to live with their disabilities.

Teaching them is the goal of Dr. Carlsen and of the staff at the school.

When parents decide Jamestown is the place for their child, the child is tested and evaluated to find out whether he or she is able to learn. If the child is accepted, the parents are required to live at the school for two weeks to see for themselves what goes on each day.

"Sometimes parents find out their child isn't as handicapped as they had thought, after they see others who have worse problems," Dr. Carlsen says. She remembers the mother of a teenage boy who had a bad limp. After she saw the severe handicaps of other students, she decided her son was not disabled. He stayed at home and went to public school.

"I believe some of the finest parents are those who have handicapped children," Dr. Carlsen says. Dr. Carlsen and the school principal have long discussions with the parents. Together they plan the type of therapy and medical help their child requires and the course of study he or she will follow. Then doctors, nurses, physical therapists, speech and occupational therapists, along with regular classroom teachers, work together to help the child develop physically, intellectually, and socially.

The school becomes home and hospital to the students. They live in dormitories, eat in the cafeteria, go down long halls to classes and

52

down other halls to therapy and treatment. They go back to their parents during Christmas and Easter and for summer vacations.

The school-home-hospital is a busy place. The course of study is almost the same as at any public school, for it is fully accredited. Besides learning to read, write, add, and subtract, however, some students must learn how to walk. Others must learn to use their hands or to speak more clearly. They must all learn to take care of themselves as much as they can with their handicaps. And they must learn to get along with the other 90 students.

Classes are very small and most teaching is on an individual basis. The teachers adapt their methods to fit the disability of each student. For those who cannot manage a pencil or a typewriter, oral assignments and exams are given. Volunteers help read lessons and copy reports. The students compete with only themselves and progress at their own rates. Often they must take time out for surgery, just as Anne did as a little girl.

There are typewriters in each classroom. Some students must type with a wand attached to a helmet.

The children get progress reports twice a year. They can stay at the school as long as they achieve.

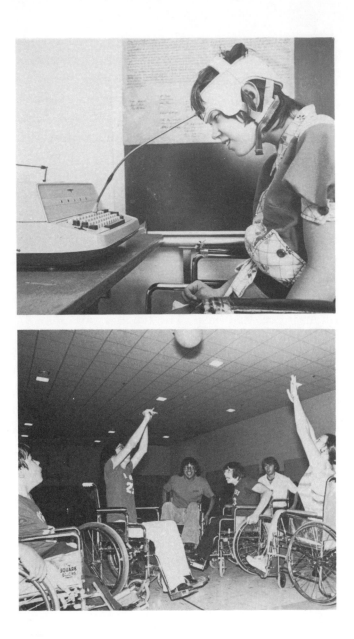

As busy as the students are, there is time for fun.

"Go, Riders, go! Go, Riders, go!" Cheers fill the gymnasium on Sunday afternoons. Basketball players dribble the ball with one hand while they push their wheelchairs toward the basket with the other.

Boys and girls from the community and from college organizations form teams to compete with the hospital-school team. They practice one hour in the wheelchairs. Then they meet the Riders in competition. The game isn't easy for them, because their hands aren't callused and they're not used to wheelchairs.

The cheerleaders are dressed in the school colors of blue and white. They wave pom-poms and lead cheers and songs from wheelchairs or leaning on crutches or sitting on the edge of the stage. Again the hospital-school team is winning! Why not? After all, they use wheelchairs every day.

Hockey, baseball, and touch football, all played from wheelchairs, are also part of the school program. Dr. Carlsen, in her enthusiasm for athletics, requires students to participate in physical education to the best of their abilities.

And there is music. Singing is a special joy for most students. Many who find it difficult to speak clearly can sing well. Concerts are given during the year for special events. At Christmas an operetta is staged. There is no school band, as most students lack the coordination necessary to play instruments, but some play the piano. Midweek chapel, usually led by a local clergyperson, is another singing time.

On Sundays a special bus, with a side door and elevator lift, takes the children to the churches of their choice in Jamestown. Going to church is often a new experience. Some students had not been able to attend home churches because they couldn't get up the steps or in and out of cars.

A number of the students, boys and girls, belong to Scout troops. As one student said, "You can camp sitting down!" Some students have gem and mineral projects. Others compete in contests in designing, essay writing, and speech.

The social event students look forward to most is the annual winter festival. Teenagers from the city of Jamestown escort the hospital-school teenagers in their wheelchairs or on their crutches. A snow queen and a snow king are crowned. Often a well-known band and soloist supply the music. After the grand march, the dancing begins. And they *all* dance. Those in wheelchairs and those on crutches move and sway to the beat, along with those who can walk and jump and move freely.

Dr. Carlsen believes her students should not be protected from life. "The more they experience in school, the easier it will be for them to get along when they are away from school," she says.

Jamestown has many curbless street crossings and ramps to make it easier for the students to wheel themselves around. Dr. Carlsen encourages the teenagers to get away from the school. They go downtown and see movies, shop, or join other Jamestown youth at the pizza houses.

Dr. Carlsen will not tolerate students using their disabilities as a way to get special treatment. On a shopping trip downtown, one teenage boy, who did not even smoke, shoplifted a package of cigarettes. Before he knew it, a police officer had taken him to the school to face Dr. Carlsen.

"What should we do about this?" asked the police officer.

"What would you do with any other child?" asked Dr. Carlsen.

"We take them to court," was the reply.

"Then he must go to court," she said.

The boy did go to court, and he faced the judge himself. He learned that neither his handicap nor Dr. Carlsen would help him get out of any trouble he made for himself. Hospital-school students take responsibility for their own actions.

Nobody Likes Every Day

Many students have never been away from home and parents before they come to Jamestown. Suddenly they find themselves surrounded by strangers. They have to work long and hard to accomplish the goals the school sets for them. Sometimes nothing seems to go right. Students become homesick and want to quit.

It was on one of these "no good" days that 13-year-old Davey decided he'd had enough of Dr. Anne and those "slave-driving" teachers. "I'm not waiting around here until summer vacation," he muttered angrily to himself. He was going home *now!*

Immediately after supper, Davey went to his dorm room. He jerked the canvas tote bag from the back of his wheelchair and tugged open the top drawer of his dresser. Into the bag he put the package of cookies his mother had just sent him. Then he reached under his socks for his money box and put that in the bag. He stowed a sweater and his Bible on top. Then he flung the bag around his neck, grabbed his crutches, and swung down the hall and out the door.

Davey found his new three-wheeler bike just where he had parked it the day before. He was the only student lucky enough to have a three-wheeler! He usually used this wonderful machine to pedal downtown or around the school campus with other students on their time off. Now he would use it to go home!

"That old cook makes me mad!" he grumbled as he hooked the tote bag over the handlebars. "Don't know how they expect a guy to eat lumpy pudding!"

It took so much strength to pedal the first 10 blocks that Davey had to eat several of his mother's cookies. Finally he turned onto the main highway and headed east. Lucky for Davey there was little traffic and the hills were gentle and rolling. Three miles he traveled.

It was getting dark. Davey put on his sweater and ate a few more cookies. Soon his bike odometer said four miles.

Davey was now tired and cold. He began to think about his warm dorm room. "Wonder if they miss me back there yet?"

Suddenly there was a loud *honk* behind him,

then screeching brakes! Davey pulled onto the gravel shoulder and watched a huge semi-truck disappear down the highway. Now he was not only cold and tired—he was frightened! He decided to go back to the school.

But as he turned around the bike tipped. Davey lost his balance. He and the bike tumbled into a low ditch. The bike landed on its side, with one wheel in the air. Davey landed on his back at the bottom of the cold, wet ditch. He could not pull himself up. As he lay there crying, all he could do was turn the wheel of the bike with one hand.

By now, the search was on. No one had ever run away from the school before! "He must be hiding somewhere around the school," Dr. Carlsen told the police officers who had been called.

A few officers went around town looking for Davey and his bike. The students made their own search around the school. The two local radio stations made announcements.

About this time, a man driving a pickup truck was heading east on the highway. As he drove by the spot Davey had fallen, the headlights of the truck picked up a turning wheel down in the ditch. The driver braked to a quick stop and scrambled down the roadway to investigate. There was Davey, wet, cold, scared, clutching his canvas bag with one hand and turning the wheel with the other.

In no time at all, Davey was back in his dorm. The students crowded around to hear about his adventure. They were all glad to have him safely back with them.

The police were astounded that Davey had pedaled more than four miles along a dark highway with no lights. "That boy has a lot of spunk!" they told Dr. Carlsen.

Dr. Carlsen agreed. She was proud of his courage and his spirit. But she also wished he hadn't tried such a dangerous journey.

"You know, Davey," she said, "you can't run away from problems. You have to face them and learn to live with them. Then, as you get older, you will find you can do almost anything you want—maybe even take a long daylight trip down a highway on your three-wheeler!"

But to be sure Davey did not try to leave again, Dr. Carlsen impounded the three-wheeler for the rest of the school year.

Travels Near and Far

Dr. Carlsen understood Davey's desperate try to go home by himself—to do what he wanted to with no help. Many times in her life she had wanted to be on her own. To be independent, to come and go when she pleased, was what Anne had always wanted. Her childhood kiddie car had helped her get around. But a grown-up woman could not use a kiddie car!

"I am going to learn to drive a car!" Dr. Carlsen declared one day. "Then I won't have to depend on anyone to take me to where I want to go."

It wasn't long before she had her own car, with a special gear shift so she could operate the car with her short arms and artificial legs. When the North Dakota State Highway Department at Bismarck heard that Dr. Anne

Carlsen intended to drive a car, a specialist was sent to Jamestown to give her the driver's exam. Soon she had passed all the tests. "I have confidence in her driving," the examiner said. "She has excellent judgment."

Dr. Carlsen had never been so free! Taking her friends for rides in her car became a Sunday afternoon event. Her favorite drive was exploring the hilly, sandy roads around Jamestown.

One rainy afternoon the sandy roads had turned to mud. This didn't stop Dr. Carlsen, even though her "excellent judgment" told her to stay on the paved roads that day. Up and down the slippery, muddy back roads they went. All of a sudden the car hit a deep hole at the bottom of a hill and stopped! They were stuck!

Dr. Carlsen tried backing up. The car didn't budge. She tried to go forward. The car didn't budge. Again and again she tried to drive out of the hole. But the spinning wheels only spattered mud over the car windows. "Now I've done it!" Anne told her friends.

"Maybe somebody will come along to push us out," they said.

"Nobody is foolish enough to be driving on these roads on a day like this!" Dr. Carlsen laughed. "We'll have to figure a way out of here ourselves."

Then her eyes fell on the two beautiful car pillows a friend had given her. There was nothing else to do!

"Take those pillows and put one in front of each back wheel," Anne told her riders. "They should give me enough traction to get out of this mud hole!"

She was right. The pillows gave the back wheels something to grab onto and the car soon lurched out of the hole. She didn't stop to rescue the ruined pillows. Afraid of becoming stuck again, she gunned the car up the hill and kept going toward the city.

Several years later, after Dr. Carlsen had been named Handicapped American of the Year, the people of Jamestown held a testimonial dinner and presented her with a brand new Mercury. This car was her pride and joy.

Dr. Carlsen's travels took her farther and farther away from the back roads around Jamestown. More and more people heard about her accomplishments. It seemed that everyone wanted to meet this amazing Anne Carlsen and hear about her work with children at the Crippled Children's School. Invitations came from all over the United States and even from other countries asking her to come and talk about the school. Dr. Carlsen accepted as many invitations as she could.

One summer she went to Venezuela in South

America to speak at a convention about her work with students with cerebral palsy. Another time she spent six weeks lecturing and visiting in Australia. She also spoke at another international meeting in Denmark. This was the homeland of her father, so she went to see the place where he had been born.

Just for fun, in 1964 Dr. Carlsen drove friends to the World's Fair in New York City. Long, long lines of people were waiting to get into the crowded, mile-square, "billion-dollar show," as it was called. Dr. Carlsen and her friends joined the slow-moving lines, leaning on crutches. They wondered if they would ever get in.

They didn't wonder long. Soon a group of Boy Scouts pushing empty wheelchairs walked along the line. "Save your feet! See the fair from a chair!" Dr. Carlsen's eyes lit up. Here was their answer!

Into the empty chairs went Dr. Carlsen and her friends. The Boy Scouts pushed them from one exhibit to the next.

As they sat in their hotel lounge that evening, another visitor to the fair sank into the chair nearest Anne.

"Whew! What a day! All that walking!" the woman exclaimed. "Aren't your feet just killing you?"

"Oh, yes, it's murder!" Dr. Carlsen agreed, with a twinkle in her eye.

Always eager to try something new at least once and always in a hurry to get somewhere, Dr. Carlsen once persuaded a Chicago pilot to give her a ride in a helicopter. "It was harder to get into that helicopter than I thought it would be," she laughed. "I couldn't step up high enough to get into it and I couldn't grab onto anything to help myself. Finally the pilot just picked me up and lifted me into the seat. The ride was worth all that, but I decided that one was enough!"

Dr. Carlsen received many invitations to speak at meetings and conventions in Washington, D.C. This became one of her favorite places to visit.

Once she took several students and staff members on a trip to the nation's capitol. When they arrived in the evening at the hotel where they'd reserved rooms, the desk clerk said, "Sorry, Dr. Carlsen. We have no vacancies and no record of reservations for your party."

The usually calm Dr. Carlsen exploded. "No reservations! You certainly do! Why, we made a deposit on these rooms long before we began the trip here!"

The nervous desk clerk called the hotel manager. Dr. Carlsen explained to him that they did have reservations and that they expected to be shown to their rooms immediately. "You aren't going to put us out on the street at this hour of the night!" she declared.

As the manager looked at this woman and her party, all using crutches or wearing braces, he knew he wouldn't put them out on the street. Rooms were found.

When Dr. Carlsen returned home and began reading her stack of mail, the letter on top was from the hotel. As she opened the envelope, a check fell out. The letter said, "Sorry, no room left for the weekend you requested. We are returning your deposit."

The desk clerk back in Washington had been right! There had been no reservations for them. But they had left Jamestown before the letter from the hotel had arrived.

The students laughed when they heard this. "Even big city hotel managers can't say no to Dr. Carlsen," they joked.

In 1964 Dr. Carlsen received an invitation to spend one year serving as a clinic coordinator at the School for Cerebral Palsied Children in Los Angeles, California. She was excited! She had spent a lot of time studying the special problems of these children. She felt she understood how to help them to learn and to become independent. This job would give her a chance to teach others how to help these children.

Anne took a leave of absence from James-

town and went to Los Angeles. Besides her
work at the clinic, she gave several talks in
California about her school and its staff in
North Dakota.

It was in Los Angeles that Anne became
acquainted with the famous musician, Law-
rence Welk, who had been born and raised in
North Dakota. "I had known of Dr. Carlsen
for a long time," Mr. Welk later said. "After
all, she was another North Dakotan. But I first
had the pleasure of meeting her personally
about 1965 when she was visiting the west
coast."

Mr. Welk arranged for Anne to talk about
herself and her work on one of his television
shows. "Everyone fell in love with her," Mr.

Welk said after her appearance on his show.

That was the beginning of a lasting friendship. Mr. Welk stops by to see Dr. Carlsen whenever he goes to North Dakota. When the school celebrated its 25th anniversary, Mr. Welk acted as honorary chairman in its appeal for funds. He helped raise thousands of dollars for the school. Since then his orchestra has played benefit concerts for the school. Mr. Welk is one of the school's loyal supporters.

"I admire Dr. Carlsen so very much," he says. "Here is a woman who had so much against her, who not only succeeded in developing herself beautifully, but is giving so much to others as well."

Many others also were impressed with the accomplishments of Dr. Carlsen. As she traveled and spoke around the country, people began to recognize her work. She was asked to serve on state and national committees dealing with education of the handicapped. She went to Washington, D.C., and testified to the Senate Subcommittee on Labor and Welfare about Bill 3102—the Physically Handicapped Children's Education Act of 1950.

Dr. Carlsen has written articles for journals dealing with the education and rehabilitation of the handicapped. She has also received achievement awards and honors. In 1958 she received the President's Trophy as the Handicapped American of the Year. She was invited to Washington, D.C., for the presentation ceremony at the annual meeting of the President's Committee on Employment of the Physically Handicapped. In 1975 she received the Gold Plate Award, given by the American Academy of Achievement. Grantsburg honored its famous hometown girl on Anne Carlsen Day in 1976.

Dr. Carlsen's portrait was painted to hang in the state capitol. The school appears in the background, with its motto, "Not to be ministered unto, but to minister." In the foreground, smiling, are two children.

Dr. Carlsen's travels have taken her a long way since the days she raced up and down the streets of Grantsburg on her kiddie car. But her favorite place to be is the school in Jamestown, surrounded by students and staff.

Anne H. Carlsen Today

"The student is Number 1 here," Dr. Carlsen tells all visitors to the school. She expects the entire staff at the school to work with this in mind, just as she does. As busy as she is in administration, she still has time for the students. They are welcome in her office when they need to talk to someone who understands.

Dr. Carlsen goes to classrooms and to therapy sessions to watch the students' progress. She sometimes eats with them in the cafeteria and visits them in their dorms. Some of the happiest memories of the alumni are of getting together with Dr. Anne in the evening to play cribbage or cards or just to talk.

One evening Dr. Carlsen and a group of students were sitting in the lounge visiting. An older girl had her arm around Dr. Carlsen's shoulder. A stranger came into the room and recognized Dr. Carlsen's face from a newspaper photo. He walked right over to her, took hold of the girl's hand and shook it, saying, "Oh, Dr. Carlsen, I'm so glad to have this chance to meet you! I've come from Minneapolis to visit your school!"

"Thank you, sir. Visitors are always welcome." Dr. Carlsen was most gracious. She smiled and answered his questions about the school. But when he was gone, everyone burst into riotous laughter. They took turns "shaking hands" with Dr. Carlsen.

Now when Dr. Carlsen goes home she only has to walk across a court to her four-room, ground-level apartment, where she lives with a friend. Dr. Carlsen is able to take care of most of her own needs. Her dresses, skirts, and shirts are made especially for her. They have front buttons and zippers she can manage by herself. She often wears capes over her shoulders instead of coats and jackets. "Blue must be your favorite color, Dr. Anne. You wear it so much!" a friend exclaimed.

"Is there any other color?" Dr. Anne laughed.

Banana splits and ice cream sundaes are her favorite foods. She belongs to the Little Pigs Club, where eating is the main activity. She will drive several miles to eat at a new restaurant or to try different food. "I suppose some people may be disturbed to have to watch me

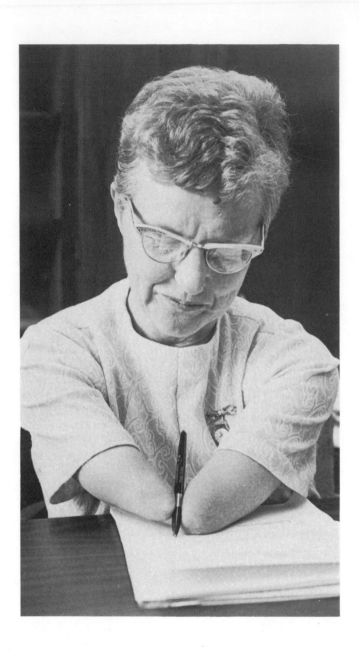

eat," she says, "but I'm used to being watched and it doesn't disturb me."

The truth is that it is very easy *not* to notice Dr. Carlsen at the table. At a wedding banquet, when the meal was almost over, a small boy sitting across the table from her suddenly said to his father, in a very loud voice, "Daddy, that lady doesn't have any hands!"

Dr. Carlsen immediately put the father at ease by saying with a smile, "No, and I don't need them, do I?" Then she picked up her cup of coffee.

When she is alone, Dr. Carlsen reads, listens to music, and watches television. But being with people is what she likes best. She belongs to a Jamestown church that has a "no steps" entrance. She plays cards with a bridge club and is active in many organizations. "When they pass the paper around for interested people to sign, I always think it is better to sign or folks will think I'm unable to write," she laughs.

This good humor and willingness to try anything once makes it fun to be around Dr. Carlsen. Friends smile when they remember a sleigh ride with her. "Better bring along a blanket for me," she said, "so I can keep my feet warm!"

Because Dr. Carlsen accepts herself and is comfortable with people, stares and thoughtless remarks from strangers usually do not bother her. Her ability to laugh at herself has saved many people from what could have been embarrassing moments.

"The handicapped need to have a healthy self-regard. They must learn that they have something to offer others," she tells people. She believes that instilling this healthy self-regard is the most important job of the school.

"Handicapped adults who feel sorry for themselves and who use their disabilities as excuses for doing nothing or for being late for jobs or for not cooperating with others or for not doing their work correctly do all of us handicapped a disservice," she says.

"No matter what the handicapped person does, he or she is going to have to put more effort into it. You have to be twice the person when you are handicapped," Dr. Carlsen says over and over to her students. "It may take a little longer and it may be more difficult, but you can do almost anything if you work at it."

As much as Dr. Carlsen believes this and is thrilled when she sees her students succeed in even the smallest of ways, she also sees children whose problems are too great for anyone to help. They may not succeed no matter how hard they try or how badly they want to. These are the students for whom Dr. Carlsen's smiles hide the sympathy she feels. It is only when she is alone that she cries for them.

Other times, the cheerfulness and confidence with which she acts as administrator, presiding over meetings, greeting visitors, listening to students, is not the way she feels inside. "Anne is only human and as such has her bad days," a long-time friend said. "She gets discouraged and depressed at times, just as we all do."

But such moments are quickly put aside. She still has much to do in preparing handicapped students to live self-sufficient and productive lives.

"Teaching here is not just a job—it is a way of life," Dr. Carlsen says. "Our teachers are very special people."

But the teachers who stay year after year do not feel special. "To be honest, I have to say that I've received as much from my students as I've given to them," the home economics teacher says, "maybe even more."

Anne Carlsen's work has helped to make the Crippled Children's Hospital-School one of the outstanding schools of its kind in the world. But Dr. Carlsen's greatest satisfaction is that more people are beginning to understand the needs and abilities of handicapped people. No longer are crippled or blind or deaf or mentally retarded children hidden away or ignored. Laws have been made which require such children to go to school. Other laws give them job opportunities and protect them from discrimination. They are being accepted for what they can do.

"Handicapped children and adults are no longer second-class citizens," Dr. Carlsen says. "If I have helped in any way to bring this about, then my work here at Jamestown has had a purpose."

YOU NEVER KNOW

You never know how far you can go in life
Until you can go no more.
You never know how bright your candle shines
Until it glows no more.

The influence you have on people
Sometimes doesn't show until you go.
And so, you never know.

—Mary Bane, 1972

Mary Bane was a student at the Crippled Children's Hospital-School. Volunteers read her lessons aloud. In her beautiful speaking voice, she dictated poems to the volunteers and to her teachers. She graduated from high school in 1974.